D1021981

DREAMS

RP Minis™
Hachette Book Group
1290 Avenue of the Americas, New York, NY 10104
www.runningpress.com
@Running_Press

Printed in the United States of America

First Edition: 02/98, Second Edition: 09/20

Published by RP Minis, an imprint of Perseus Books, LLC, a subsidiary of Hachette Book Group, Inc. The RP Minis name and logo is a trademark of the Hachette Book Group.

The Hachette Speakers Bureau provides a wide range of authors for speaking events. To find out more, go to www.hachettespeakersbureau.com or call (866) 376-6591.

The publisher is not responsible for websites (or their content) that are not owned by the publisher.

Design by Amanda Richmond

Library of Congress Control Number: 2020931586

ISBN: 978-0-7624-9796-6

LREX

10 9 8 7 6 5 4 3 2 1

DREAMS

A LITTLE INTRODUCTION TO THE SYMBOLS

Illustrated by Mara Penny

RP MINIS

PHILADELPHIA

THE
SYMBOLS

ACORN

Seeing acorns in a dream
predicts pleasant things ahead
and that much gain is to be
expected. To pick them from the
ground foretells success after
weary labors. To shake them
from trees denotes that you will
rapidly attain your wishes in
business or love.

ANGELS

When wicked people dream of angels it is a demand to repent; to good people it should be a consolation. If the dream is unusually pleasing, you will hear of the health of friends and receive a legacy from an unknown relative.

APPLES

To see red apples on trees with green foliage is exceedingly fortunate for the dreamer. Ripe apples denote that the time has arrived for you to realize your hopes. Think over what you intend to do and go fearlessly ahead. A ripe apple on top of a tree warns you not to aim too high.

ARROW

Pleasure follows this dream.
Entertainments, festivals,
and pleasant journeys may be
expected. Suffering will cease.

BEAR

A bear signifies overwhelming competition in pursuits of every kind. To kill a bear foretells liberation from former entanglements.

BED

A clean, white bed denotes a peaceful end of worries. To dream that you are sleeping on a bed in the open air foretells that you will have delightful experiences and opportunities for improving your future.

BICYCLE

To dream of riding a bicycle
uphill signifies bright prospects.
Riding downhill calls for care—
misfortune hovers near.

BIRTHDAY GIFTS

Receiving happy
surprises signifies many
high accomplishments.
Working people will
advance in their trades.

BUTTERFLY

To see a butterfly among flowers and green grasses indicates prosperity and fair attainments. To see butterflies flying about denotes news from absent friends by letter or from someone who has seen them.

CANDY

To dream of making candy
denotes profit accruing from
industry. To dream of eating
crisp, new candy implies social
pleasures and much lovemaking
among the young and old.

CANDLES

To see candles burning with a clear and steady flame denotes the constancy of those around you, and a well-grounded fortune. For a young person to dream that they are molding candles indicates that they will have an unexpected offer of marriage and a pleasant visit to distant relatives. If they are lighting a candle, they will meet their

lover clandestinely because
of parental objections.

CHERUBS

To dream of cherubs
foretells that you will have
some distinct joy, which will
leave an impression of lasting
good upon your life.

CROWN

To dream of a crown predicts
a change of mode in the habit
of one's life. The dreamer will
travel a long distance from
home and form new relations.
To dream of crowning a person
shows your own worthiness.

DANCE

To dream of seeing a crowd
of merry children dancing
signifies loving, obedient,
and intelligent children and a
cheerful and comfortable home.
To young people it denotes
easy tasks and many pleasures.
To see older people dancing
foretells a brighter outlook for
business. To dream that you
are dancing means that some

unexpected good fortune
will come to you.

DAYBREAK

To watch the day break in a
dream is an omen of successful
undertakings. But if the scene
is indistinct and weird, it may
imply disappointment when
success in business or
love seems assured.

DIAMONDS

To dream of owning diamonds
is a very promising dream
signifying great honor and
recognition from high places.
Diamonds are omens of good
luck, unless stolen from the
bodies of dead persons. If that
occurs, they foretell that your
own unfaithfulness will be
discovered by your friends.

DUCKS

To dream of seeing wild
ducks on a clear stream of
water signifies fortunate
journeys, perhaps across the
sea. To see ducks flying foretells a brighter future for you.
It also denotes marriage and
children in a new home.

DYNAMITE

To see dynamite in a dream
is a sign of approaching
change and the expanding
of one's affairs.

EAGLES

To see an eagle soaring
above you denotes lofty
ambitions which you will
struggle fiercely to realize;
nevertheless, you will gain your
desires. To see an eagle perched
on distant heights predicts
that you will possess fame,
wealth, and the highest position
available in your country.

EARRINGS

To see earrings in dreams is
an omen that good news and
interesting work are before you.

ELEPHANTS

To dream of riding an
elephant denotes that you will
possess wealth and honors,

which you will wear with dignity. You will rule absolutely in business affairs and your word will be law in the home. Many elephants denote prosperity. One lone elephant signifies that you will live in a small but solid way. Feeding an elephant foretells that you will elevate yourself in your community by your kindness.

EVERGREEN

This dream brings boundless
resources of wealth, happiness,
and learning. It is an indication
of future prosperity.

FAWN

To dream of seeing a
fawn denotes that you will
have true and upright friends.
To the young it indicates
faithfulness in love.

FEATHERS

To dream of seeing feathers falling around you denotes that your burden in life will be light and easily borne. To see eagle feathers predicts that your aspirations will be realized. To see chicken feathers denotes small annoyances.

FINGERS

To see well-kept nails
indicates scholarly tastes
and literary success.

FIRE

Fire is favorable to the dreamer if they do not get burned. To dream that your home is burning denotes a loving companion, obedient children, and careful servants. To dream that a store is burning foretells a great rush in business and profitable results.

FROGS

To see frogs in a dream
signifies that you will
have a pleasant and even-
tempered friend as your
confidant and counselor.

GLOVES

To dream of wearing new gloves denotes that you will be cautious and economical in your dealings with others. You will have lawsuits or business troubles, but you will settle them in a manner that satisfies you. To find a pair of gloves denotes a marriage or new love affair.

GOBLET

To see goblets of ancient
design means that you
will receive favors and
benefits from strangers.

GRAPES

If you see grapes growing in
abundance among leaves,
you will soon attain eminent
positions and be able to impart
happiness to others. For a young
person this dream is one of
bright promise. They will have
their most ardent wish granted.

GRASS

This is a very fortunate dream indeed. It gives a promise of a happy and well advanced life to the tradesperson, rapid accumulation of wealth, fame to artistic and literary people, and a safe voyage through the turbulent sea of love.

HAT

For a man to dream that
he wears a new hat predicts a
change of place and business
which will be very much to
his advantage. For a woman to
dream that she wears a fine new
hat denotes the attainment of
wealth and that she will be the
object of much admiration.

For the wind to blow off
your hat denotes a sudden
change in affairs.

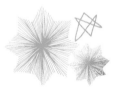

HENS

To dream of hens predicts
pleasant family reunions
with added members.

HONEY

To dream of eating honey
foretells that you will attain
wealth and love. To lovers this
indicates a swift rush into
marital joys.

HORSE

If you dream of seeing or riding
a white horse, it is an indication
of prosperity and pleasurable
commingling with friends. To
dream of dark horses signifies
prosperous conditions but a
large amount of discontent.

HOUSE

If you dream of building a
house, you will make wise
changes in your present affairs.
To dream that you own an
elegant house denotes that you
will soon leave your home
for a better one and that
fortune will be kind to you.

ICE CREAM

To dream that you are eating ice
cream foretells happy success in
affairs already undertaken. To
see children eating it predicts
that prosperity and happiness
will attend you most favorably.

ISLAND

To see an island is symbolic of comfort and easy circumstances after much striving and worrying to meet honorable obligations. To see people on an island denotes a struggle to raise yourself higher in prominent circles.

IVY

To dream of seeing ivy
growing on trees or houses
predicts excellent health
and an increase of fortune.
Innumerable joys will
succeed this dream.

JEWELS

To dream of jewels denotes
much pleasure and riches.
To wear them brings rank
and satisfied ambitions. If
you see others wearing them,
distinguished places will be held
by you or some friend.

JOCKEY

To dream of a jockey is an omen
that you will appreciate a gift
from an unexpected source.
To see a jockey thrown from a
horse signifies that strangers
will call upon you for aid.

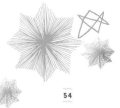

JURY

To dream that you are on a jury
denotes dissatisfaction with your
employment and that you will seek
to change your position. If you are
cleared from a charge by a jury,
your business will be successful
and affairs will move your way,
but if you should be condemned,
enemies will overpower you and
harass you beyond endurance.

KANGAROO

To see a kangaroo in your dreams means that you will outwit a wily enemy who seeks to place you in an unfavorable position before the public.

KEYS

To dream of keys denotes
unexpected change. If the keys
are lost, unpleasant adventures
will affect you. To find keys
brings domestic peace and
brisk turns to business.

KISS

To see children kissing means that happy reunions in families and satisfactory work will follow. To dream that you kiss your mother predicts that you will be very successful in your enterprises and be honored and beloved by your friends. To kiss your sweetheart in the dark denotes dangers and immoral

engagements. To kiss your
lover in the light signifies
honorable intentions.

LACE

If you dream of lace, you will
be happy in the realization of
your most ambitious desires
and lovers will bow to your
command without questioning.

LADDER

To dream of a ladder
being raised for you to ascend
predicts that energetic and
nervy qualifications will
raise you to prominence in
business affairs. To ascend a
ladder means prosperity and
uninterrupted happiness.

LAMB

To dream of lambs frolicking
in green pastures signifies
chaste friendships and joys,
bounteous and profitable crops
to farmers, and increase of
possessions for others. A lost
lamb means that wayward
people will be under
your influence.

LETTERS

To dream often of receiving
a letter from a friend
foretells their arrival or that
you will hear from them
by letter or otherwise.

LION

To dream of a lion signifies
that a great force is driving
you. If you subdue the lion,
you will be victorious in any
engagement. If it overpowers
you, you will be open to the
successful attacks of enemies.

MONEY

To dream of finding
money denotes small
worries but much happiness.
Changes will follow.

MOON

To dream of seeing the moon
with the aspect of the heavens
remaining normal is an omen
of success in love and business
affairs. To see the new moon
denotes an increase in wealth
and congenial partners
in marriage.

MOUNTAIN

If you ascend a mountain in your dreams and the way is pleasant and verdant, you will rise to wealth and prominence. If the mountain is rugged and you fail to reach the top, you may expect reverses in your life. To awaken when you are at a dangerous point in ascending indicates that you will find affairs taking a flattering turn.

MUSIC

To dream of hearing
harmonious music is an omen
of pleasure and prosperity.
Discordant music foretells
troubles with unruly children.

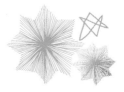

NAKED

To dream that you suddenly discover your nudity and are trying to conceal it denotes that you have sought illicit pleasure, contrary to your noblest instincts, and are desirous of abandoning those desires.

NEEDLE

To find a needle predicts
that you will have friends
who appreciate you.
To look for a needle
foretells useless worries.

NIGHTINGALE

To dream that you are
listening to the pleasant
notes of the nightingale
signifies a pleasing existence
and prosperous and healthy
surroundings. This is a
most favorable dream to
lovers and parents.

NOSE

To see your own nose
indicates force of character and
consciousness of your ability to
accomplish whatever enterprise
you may choose to undertake.

NURSE

To see a nurse leaving
your house is an omen of good
health in the family.

OATMEAL

To dream of eating oatmeal
signifies the enjoyment of
worthily earned fortune. For
a young person to dream of
preparing it for the table means
that they will soon preside over
the destiny of others.

OCEANS

It is hopeful to dream of the ocean when it is calm. The sailor will have a pleasant and profitable voyage, those in business will enjoy a season of remuneration, and the young person will revel in their sweetheart's charms.

ONIONS

If you eat onions in a dream, you will overcome all opposition. If you see them growing, there will be just enough rivalry in your affairs to make things interesting.

ORGAN

To hear the pealing forth of an organ in grand anthems signifies lasting friendships and well-grounded fortune. If you dream of rendering harmonious music on an organ you will be fortunate in the way of worldly comfort and much social distinction will be given you.

PALM TREE

Palm trees seen in your
dreams are messages of
hopeful situations and
happiness of a high order.

PARK

To dream of walking
through a well-kept park
denotes enjoyable leisure.
If you walk with your lover,
you will be comfortably
and happily married.

PEARLS

To dream of pearls is a fore-runner of good business, trade, and affairs of a social nature. If a young woman dreams that her lover sends her gifts of pearls, she will indeed be most fortunate. There will be occasions of festivity and pleasure for her, along with a loving and faithful engagement without the jealous inclinations so ruinous to the peace of lovers.

PIG

To dream of a fat,
healthy pig indicates
reasonable success in affairs.

POTATOES

Dreaming of potatoes brings incidents of good. To dream of digging them denotes success. To dream of eating them means that you will enjoy substantial gain. To cook them foretells pleasant employment. Planting potatoes brings realization of desires.

QUAKER

To dream of a Quaker denotes
that you will have faithful
friends and fair business. If you
dream that you are a Quaker,
you will conduct yourself
honorably toward an enemy.

QUEEN

To dream of a queen foretells
successful ventures. If she looks
old or haggard, there will be
disappointments connected
with your pleasures.

QUILTS

To dream of quilts foretells
pleasant and comfortable
circumstances.

RABBITS

To dream of rabbits
foretells a favorable turn in
conditions. You will be more
pleased with your gains than
you were formerly. To see white
rabbits signifies faithfulness
in love to the married or single.
To see rabbits frolicking about
denotes that children will
contribute to your joys.

RAINBOW

To see a rainbow in a
dream predicts unusual
happenings. Affairs will assume
a more promising countenance
and crops will give promise of a
plentiful yield. For lovers to
see the rainbow is an omen

of much happiness in their
union. To see the rainbow
hanging low over green trees
signifies unconditional
success in any undertaking.

REINDEER

To dream of a reindeer
signifies faithful duty and
loyalty to friends.

ROSES

To dream of seeing roses
blooming and fragrant denotes
that some joyful occasion is
nearing and you will possess the
faithful love of your sweetheart.
To inhale their fragrance
brings unalloyed pleasure.

SLIPPERS

To dream that your slippers are
much admired foretells that you
will be involved in a flirtation
that will bring disgrace.

SOAP

To dream of soap foretells
that friendships will
reveal interesting
entertainment. Farmers
will have success in
their varied affairs.

SQUIRREL

To dream of seeing squirrels
means that pleasant friends
will soon visit you. You will
also see advancement in
your business. To pet one
signifies family joy.

STARS

To dream of looking upon
clear, shining stars foretells
good health and prosperity.
If you dream of stars appearing
and vanishing mysteriously,
there will be some strange
changes and happenings
in your near future.

SUN

To dream of seeing a clear,
shining sunrise signifies joyous
events and prosperity. To see
the sun at noontide denotes
the maturity of ambitions and
signals unbounded satisfaction.

A sun shining through
clouds indicates that troubles
and difficulties are losing
their hold on you and that
prosperity is nearing.

SWANS

To dream of seeing white
swans floating upon placid
waters foretells prosperous
outlooks and delightful
experiences. To see a black
swan denotes illicit pleasure.

TEA

To dream that you
are thirsty for tea means that
you will be surprised with
uninvited guests.

THEATER

To dream of being at
a theater prophesizes that you
will have much pleasure in the
company of new friends. Your
affairs will be satisfactory after
this dream. If you are one
of the players, your pleasures
will be of short duration.

TOMATOES

To dream of eating tomatoes
signals the approach of
good health. To see them
growing denotes domestic
enjoyment and happiness.
For a young woman to see
a ripe tomato foretells her
happiness in the married state.

TURTLE

To dream of seeing turtles
signifies that an unusual
incident will bring you
enjoyment and improve
your business conditions.
To drink turtle soup denotes
that you will find pleasure in
compromising intrigue.

TOWER

To dream of seeing a tower
denotes that you will aspire
to high elevations. If you
climb one you will
succeed in your wishes.

UMBRELLA

To carry a new umbrella
over you in a clear shower
or sunshine is an omen
of exquisite pleasure and
prosperity. To see others
carrying them foretells that
you will be appealed to
for aid by charity.

UNIFORM

To see a uniform in your
dream means that you will
have influential friends to aid
you in obtaining your desires.

VEGETABLES

To dream of eating
vegetables is an omen
of strange luck.

VEIL

To dream that you wear a veil
foretells that you will not be
perfectly sincere with your
lover and will be forced to use
trickery to retain them.

VINEYARD

To dream of a vineyard denotes
favorable investments and
auspicious love-making.

VIOLETS

To see violets in your
dreams, or gather them,
brings joyous occasions in
which you will find favor
with some superior person.

VIOLIN

To see or hear a violin
in dreams foretells harmony
and peace in the family
and that financial affairs
will cause no apprehension.

WALTZ

To see the waltz danced
suggests that you will have
pleasant relations
with a cheerful and
adventuresome person.

WATER

To play in the water denotes
a sudden awakening to love
and passion. To have it
sprayed on your head
denotes that your passionate
awakening to love will meet
reciprocal consummation.

WATERFALL

To dream of a waterfall
foretells that you will secure
your wildest desire and that
fortune will be exceedingly
favorable to your progress.

WAVES

To dream of waves is a sign
that you hold some vital step
in contemplation; if the
waves are clear, that step will
result in much knowledge.

WINE

To dream of drinking wine predicts joy and consequent friendships. To dream of breaking bottles of wine foretells that your love and passion will border on excess. To see barrels of wine is symbolic of great luxury. To pour it from one vessel into another signifies that your enjoyments will be varied and that you will journey to many notable places.

YARN

To dream of yarn denotes
success in business and an
industrious companion
in your home.

ZEBRA

To dream of a zebra
predicts that you will be
interested in varying and
fleeting enterprises.

ZODIAC

To study the zodiac in your dreams means that you will gain distinction and favor through your intercourse with strangers. If you approach it or it approaches you, you will succeed in your endeavors to the wonderment of others and beyond your wildest imagination. To draw a map of it signifies future gain.

This book is bound using
handcraft methods, and is
Smyth-sewn to ensure durability.

The book was illustrated
by Mara Penny.

The book was designed
by Amanda Richmond.

The text was edited by
Jenny Comita and
Shannon Fabricant.